The Wisdom of the

The Wisdom of the

Compiled and Edited by Jim Gallery

WALNUT GROVE PRESS
Nashville, TN 37211

ISBN 1-887655-99-9

The ideas expressed in this book are not, in all cases, exact quotations, as some have been edited for clarity and brevity. In all cases, the author has attempted to maintain the speaker's original intent. In some cases, material for this book was obtained from secondary sources, primarily print media. While every effort was made to ensure the accuracy of these sources, the accuracy cannot be guaranteed. For additions, deletions, corrections or clarifications in future editions of this text, please write WALNUT GROVE PRESS.

Printed in the United States of America
1 2 3 4 5 6 7 8 9 10 • 99 00 01 02 03 04 05

Cover Design & Layout: Bart Dawson
Typesetting: Sue Gerdes

ACKNOWLEDGMENTS
The author gratefully acknowledges the helpful support of Criswell Freeman, Eloise Gallery, and Daphne Megaw.

For my sisters, Patti and Jan

Joint heirs to a wonderful Irish heritage

Table of Contents

Introduction

Holidays were always special when I was growing up. St. Patrick's Day was one of the best. Memories of my Dad wearing a funny green hat and issuing Irish proclamations, usually nonsensical and humorous, still bring celebration to my soul.

The Irish are a celebrative, joyful people who live life to the fullest. I am thankful for my Irish heritage and for the contributions the Irish have made to the history of the world.

After a leisurely stroll through these pages of inspirational quotes, toasts, and blessings, I trust you too will thank your lucky four-leaf clover for the wisdom of the Irish. Whether you are Irish, adopted Irish, or just appreciative of the Irish culture, you will find this book uplifting and encouraging.

So sit back, put on a "wee bit o' green," and learn from the wit and wisdom of the Irish. And maybe, just maybe, if you are quick enough, you will see a leprechaun who will lead you to your very own "pot o' gold."

The Land and the People

The mystique of the Emerald Isle and her people is enhanced by the remarkable beauty of the land itself. Bookstores are filled with picture essays of green countrysides and lush landscapes. World photographers are captivated by the land and people of Ireland, and with good cause: The Irish countryside is like no other place on earth.

Over the centuries, writers have prosaically and poetically captured the world's collective imagination with descriptions of this picturesque land. In this chapter, through the words of notable Irishmen and women, we take an imaginary journey to the land of leprechauns.

Ireland is a bit of heaven.

J. Keith Brennan

It's the one place on earth
That heaven has kissed
With melody, mirth
And meadow and mist.

Irish Blessing

God made the grass, the air, and the rain;
and the grass, the air and the rain made
the Irish; and the Irish turned the grass,
the air and the rain back to God.

Sean O'Faolain

O, Ireland, isn't it grand you look
Like a bride in her rich adornin'?
And with all the pent-up love of my heart
I bid you the top o' the morning!

John Locke

Ireland was born on a storm-swept rock and
hates the soft growth of sun-baked lands
where there is no frost in men's bones.

Liam O'Flaherty

Ireland is a country
in which the probable
never happens and the
impossible always does.

John P. Mahaffy

Ireland is The Land of Youth.

George W. Russell

How sweetly lies old Ireland
Emerald green beyond the foam.
Awakening sweet memories,
Calling the heart back home.

Irish Blessing

This island is endowed with so many dowries
of nature, considering the fruitlessness
of the soil.

Francis Bacon

The real beauty of Ireland is
much more than skin-deep.

Kate O'Brien

If you are lucky enough
to be Irish, you're
lucky enough.

Grace Boyle

To be Irish is to be twice blessed: first as a life, then as a "liver" of life.

Bridget O'Donnell

The Irish, when good, are perfect.

Lord Byron

Nothing's too good for the Irish.

Irish-American Saying

Irishmen are the Texans of Europe.

Anonymous

Everybody's Irish on St. Patrick's Day.

Helen O'Donnell Malloy

Irish Blessings

The Irish people have a well-earned reputation for celebration: Irishmen enjoy life to the fullest. And when the Irish feel the need to celebrate, they do so with family and friends. An important part of many such occasions is the Irish blessing.

Enjoy the blessings that follow. They reflect the love for life that is the hallmark of those special people who call Ireland home.

May your blessings
outnumber the
shamrocks that grow.
And may trouble
avoid you
wherever
you go.

Irish Blessing

These things I warmly
wish for you —
Someone to love,
Some work to do,
A bit o' sun,
A bit o' cheer,
And a guardian angel
Always near.

Old Irish Greeting

May your troubles be less,
And your blessings be more,
And nothing but happiness
Come through your door.

Irish Blessing

May brooks and trees and singing hills
join in the chorus too, and every gentle wind
that blows send happiness to you.

Irish Blessing

May you never find trouble
All crowdin' and shovin'
But always good fortune —
All smilin' and lovin'.

Irish Blessing

May you always have these blessings:
A soft breeze when summer comes,
A warm fireside in winter —
And always — the warm, soft smile of a friend.

Irish Blessing

Grant me a sense
of humor, Lord,
The saving grace
to see a joke,
To win some
happiness from life,
And pass it on
to other folk.

Irish Blessing

May you be half-an-hour
in Heaven before the
Devil knows you're dead.

Irish Blessing

May the luck of the Irish be always at hand
And good friends always near you —
May each and every coming day
Bring some special joy to cheer you.

Irish Blessing

May you have all the happiness
And luck that life can hold,
And at the end of all your rainbows
May you find a pot of gold.

Irish Blessing

God needed laughter in the world,
So he made the Irish race,
For they can meet life with a smile
And turn a happy face.

Irish Blessing

May the hinges
of our friendship
never grow rusty.

Irish Blessing

Let's all put on our dancin' shoes
And wear our shamrocks green
And toast our friends both here and there
And everywhere between.

Irish Toast

May the luck of the Irish
Lead to happiest heights
And the highway you travel
Be lined with green lights!

Irish Blessing

May leprechauns
strew happiness
Wherever you walk
each day
And Irish angels
smile on you
All along the way.

Irish Blessing

Bless your little Irish heart
and every other
Irish part.

Irish Blessing

May you never
forget what is worth
remembering, or
remember what
is best forgotten.

Irish Blessing

May you have the hindsight
to know where you have been,
And the foresight to know
where you are going,
And the insight to know
when you have gone too far.
In the name of God who
made a pathway of waves,
May he bring us safely
home at the end of the day.

Irish Blessing

May good luck be always your friend
through life in all that you do,
And may trouble be always
a stranger to you.

Irish Blessing

Like the warmth of the sun
And the light of the day,
May the luck of the Irish
Shine bright on your way.

Irish Blessing

To wish you the luck
o' the Irish, begorra!
Not just for today
But for every tomorra!

Irish Blessing

3

The Luck of the Irish

Much has been made of the luck of the Irish: Legends and myths amuse us with tales of good fortune miraculously falling upon some unsuspecting soul. These tales make for good reading and pleasant diversions, but in truth, a staunch work ethic characterizes the Irish more than plain old luck. History records the Irish as a hard-working people who deserved any break that came their way.

Herein, we consider ways to make your own luck. Pick a shamrock or two; kiss the Blarney Stone if you must; but first roll up your sleeves and get to work. It's the Irish way.

Luck means the long nights you have devoted
to work; luck means the appointments you have
never failed to keep; luck means the trains
you have never failed to catch.

Max O'Rell

There is a silent dignity, a fundamental
usefulness, a primeval necessity in work.

Father Flanagan

Things do not happen.
They are made to happen.

John F. Kennedy

Your luck is how
you treat people.

Bridget O'Donnell

In the matter of ideas,
    he who meditates is lost.

William McFee

Look at your choices, pick the best one,
    then go to work with all your heart.

Pat Riley

The only way to get positive feelings about
yourself is to take positive actions. Man does
not live as he thinks; he thinks as he lives.

Reverend Vaughan Quinn

The Higher the ideal,
the more work is required
to accomplish it. Do not
expect to become a great
success in life if you are
not willing to work for it.

Father Flanagan

Never confuse a single mistake
with a final mistake.

F. Scott Fitzgerald

Tragedy is a tool for the living to gain wisdom,
not a guide by which to live.

Robert Kennedy

Never despair, but if you do,
work on in despair.

Edmund Burke

You always pass failure on the way to success.

Mickey Rooney

Too much idleness leaves
a man less his own master
than any sort
of employment.

Edmund Burke

Laziness is a heavy load.

Irish Proverb

What you can't get out of,
    get into whole-heartedly.

Mignon McLaughlin

A goal is a dream with a deadline.

Harvey MacKay

No boy's education is complete until he has been taught to accept nothing from life except what he can win with his own hands. We all must work. We all have some job to do.

Father Flanagan

If your play interrupts your work, you're healthy. If work interrupts your play, you're broke.

James (Big Jim) O'Hara

We need above all to learn again to believe in the possibility of nobility of spirit in ourselves.

Eugene O'Neill

One man with a dream,
at pleasure, shall go forth
and conquer a crown....

Arthur William Edgar O'Shaughnessy

Let us go forth asking
His help and His blessing
but knowing that here
on earth, God's work
must truly be our own.

John F. Kennedy

She didn't know it couldn't be done, so she went ahead and did it.

Bridget O'Donnell

The days you work
are the best days.

Georgia O'Keefe

Life

The Irish people love life. Perhaps this fact helps explain the world's unending love affair with the Irish. Irishmen don't simply live, they *enjoy* living, and they're never bashful about sharing their joy with others. Irish enthusiasm, it seems, is always contagious. In this chapter, Irishmen and women share their insights on life. Enjoy!

Don't hurry. Don't worry.
You're only here for
a short visit. So don't
forget to stop and
smell the roses.

Walter Hagan

Happiness is the harvest of a quiet eye.

Austen O'Malley

Life is half-spent before
we know what it is.

Irish Proverb

A life without love is like Ireland without springtime.

Irish Proverb

Many people think they are taking life seriously when they are only taking themselves seriously.

Joseph T. O'Callahan

He who takes himself seriously is overly conscious of his rights. He who takes life seriously is fully conscious of his obligations.

Joseph T. O'Callahan

Adversity is a severe instructor,
set over us by one who knows us better
than we know ourselves.

Edmund Burke

The time to repair the roof
is when the sun is shining.

John F. Kennedy

The important thing is to learn a lesson
every time you lose.

John McEnroe

God never shuts one door unless He opens another.

Irish Proverb

Character is formed by doing the thing we are supposed to do, when it should be done, whether we feel like doing it or not.

Father Flanagan

Character is the choices a human being
makes under pressure.

Robert McKee

Character development is the great,
if not the sole, aim of education.

William O'Shea

Your thorns are the best part of you.

Marianne Moore

You are the architect of
your personal experience.

Shirley MacLaine

Don't let other people
tell you what you want.

Pat Riley

It is twice as hard to crush a half-truth
as a whole lie.

Austin O'Malley

Truth lives in the cellar; error on the doorstep.

Austin O'Malley

A tune is more lasting
than the song of birds.
And a word is more lasting
than the wealth
of the world.

Irish Proverb

Man's loneliness is but
his fear of life.

Eugene O'Neill

Making your unknown known is the important thing — and keeping the unknown always beyond you.

Georgia O'Keefe

Welcome, O life! I go to
encounter for the millionth
time the reality
of your experience.

James Joyce

Religion

Religion is an integral part of any culture and the Irish culture is no exception. A passionate, hard-working, hard-playing people must find a source of strength beyond themselves. The Irish people have turned to God as that strength. Whether through the Protestant tradition or the Catholic, Irish men and women know from whence cometh their help. Perhaps a wee bit more of that old-time religion — Irish style — would do us all some good.

Without God at the beginning there can only be confusion at the end.

Father Flanagan

Man is born broken.
He lives by mending.
The grace of God
is the glue.

Eugene O'Neill

We look for God as though
he were not already here.

Merritt Malloy

When men make God, there is no God.

Eugene O'Neill

Without religious faith there can be
no lasting enthusiasm. Man cannot lift himself
by tugging at his own bootstraps.

Father Flanagan

If you want faith, you have to work for it.

Flannery O'Connor

You're not free until
you've been made captive
by supreme belief.

Marianne Moore

There is nothing that God has judged good for us that he has not given us the means to accomplish.

Edmund Burke

God often pays debts
without money.

Irish Proverb

Woe to him who is not content with having God as his sustenance.

Irish Proverb

Faith and work make a
triumphant combination.

Father Flanagan

Passion

The Irish are blamed for many a tantrum; any spark of anger can be labeled as an "Irish temper." But the Irish don't have temper problems so much as they have a passion for life. They place their whole hearts into their endeavors whether at work or play. The Irish are, in short, a people who live — and love — with passion.

In a world characterized by the status quo and by mediocrity, the Irish have much to teach us. For a dose of Irish intensity, turn the page…and brace yourself!

The Irish, with their glowing hearts, are needed in this age.

Lydia Maria Child

The world belongs
to the enthusiast who
keeps his cool.

William McFee

A tie is like kissing your sister.

Duffy Daugherty

Success is not so much achievement as achieving. Refuse to join the cautious crowd that plays not to lose. Play to win.

David J. Mahoney

Only those who risk greatly can achieve greatly.

Robert Kennedy

Sometimes it's risky not to take a risk.

Harvey MacKay

A young person should never be made to feel that no great thing is expected of him or her.

Father Flanagan

When anyone asks me about the Irish character, I say: "Look at the trees: maimed, stark, and misshapen, but ferociously tenacious."

Edna O'Brien

If fate means you to lose,
  give him a good fight anyhow.

        William McFee

There is no great loss
  without some small profit.

        Irish Proverb

Those wild Irish.

        Robert Burton

A timid man is never far from danger.

        Irish Proverb

A poor heart is poorer
than a poor purse.

Irish Proverb

Irishmen have
the best hearts.

Horace Walpole

Our Irish blunders
are never blunders
of the heart.

Maria Edgeworth

A kind heart never loses
in the end.

Irish Proverb

What is nearest the heart is usually
nearest the lips.

Irish Proverb

Let you courage guard your future.

Finlay McKenna

Do not ask the Lord for riches;
ask Him for courage.

Irish Proverb

What you can't get out of, get into whole-heartedly.

Mignon McLaughlin

Good order is the foundation of all things.

Edmund Burke

Order is exotic in Ireland. It has been imported from England, but will not grow.

J. A. Froude

I am troubled;
I'm dissatisfied:
I'm Irish.

Marianne Moore

Toasts

The Irish people know how — and where — to relax: in pubs. The Irish pub has been a gathering place for centuries; a place where yarns are spun, legends begun, and most of all, where friends are found.

Toasts reflect the closeness of the Irish people and their propensity for good cheer. So lift your glass or cup and offer up a toast like a true Irishman. Here's how...

Here's to a light heart
and the heavy hand.

Irish Toast

May we always have a clean shirt, a clean conscience, and a bob in the pocket.

Irish Toast

Here's to the health of your enemies' enemies.

Irish Toast

May the dust of your carriage wheels
blind the eyes of your foes.

Irish Toast

May your enemies have short shoes
and long corns.

Irish Toast

May the roof above us
never fall in, and may we
friends gathered below
never fall out.

Irish Toast

We drink to your coffin. May it be built from the wood of a hundred-year-old oak tree that I shall plant tomorrow!

Irish Toast

Here's to health, peace, and prosperity;
May the flower of Love never be
nipped by the frost of disappointment,
Nor shadow of grief fall among
your family or friends.

Irish Toast

May peace and plenty be the first
to lift the latch on your door,
And happiness be guided to your home
by the candle of Christmas.

Irish Toast

Long live the Irish!
Long live their cheer!
Long live our friendship,
year after year!

Irish Toast

May you have warm words on a cold evening, a full moon on a dark night, and a road downhill all the way to your door.

Irish Toast

Here's to a wet night
and a dry morning.

Irish Toast

May you live all the days
of your life.

Irish Toast

May you live to be a
hundred years old...
with one extra year
to repent.

Irish Toast

Humor

The Irish understand that a good laugh is good medicine and that laughter makes a happy home. It's no surprise, then, that the Irish can laugh at a good joke — and at themselves.

In this chapter, feel free to enjoy a few chuckles at the expense of the Irish. They don't mind; in fact, they're probably laughing, too.

We Irishmen are banking heavily on the fact that God has a sense of humor.

Jim Murray

The Irish don't know
what they want and
are prepared to fight
to the death to get it.

Sidney Littlewood

It is better to be quiet and ignorant that
to open your mouth and remove all doubt.

John McNamara

It is almost as important to know
what is not serious as to know what is.

John Kenneth Galbraith

The more you strive to be sensible and
serious and meaningful, the less chance you
have of becoming so. The primary objective
is to laugh.

John D. MacDonald

The best way to get a husband to do anything
is to suggest that perhaps he's too old to do it.

Shirley MacLaine

Hard work never killed
anybody, but why take
the chance.

Charlie McCarthy

The English should give
Ireland home rule —
but reserve the
motion picture rights.

Will Rogers

Other people have a nationality. The Irish have a psychosis.

Brendan Behan

I'm the only Irishman who never made a speech.

George Moore

In some parts of Ireland, the sleep that knows no waking is always followed by the wake that knows no sleeping.

Mary Wilson Little

An Irishman is a guy
who believes everything
he can't see—and nothing
he can.

Jim Murray

God created whiskey so
that the Irish would not
conquer the world.

Irish Saying

A man who can't laugh
at himself should be
given a mirror!

Irish Saying

Poets and Romantics

The Irish are a passionate people who work and play with gusto. So it's not surprising that the Irish boast more than their fair share of poets, minstrels and writers. The wild Irish heart, it seems, must find expression.

The following quotations describe the romance and creativity that are the hallmarks of the Irish spirit. Long may that spirit live!

Irish are poets. They talk about their souls and mists and so on.

P.G. Wodehouse

Every St Patrick's Day,
every Irishman goes out
to find another Irishman
to make a speech to.

Shane Leslie

For me, singing sad songs often has a way
of healing a situation. It gets the hurt out in
the open — into the light, out of the darkness.

Reba McEntire

Music, melody, and rhythm find their way
into the secret places of the soul, radiating joy.

Father Flanagan

Music heals everything but a toothache.

Irish Proverb

Irish is English
set to music.

Mary Michael Malloy

Birds sing after a storm.
Why shouldn't we?

Rose Fitzgerald Kennedy

There is wisdom in the habit of looking at the bright side of life.

Father Flanagan

Love isn't just doing good things. Love is
the spirit with which we do good things.

Merritt Malloy

Love is a verb.

Merritt Malloy

The human heart, at whatever age,
opens only to the heart that opens in return.

Maria Edgeworth

The Irish men are
reckoned terrible
heart-stealers.

Mary Wollstonecraft

Isn't sacrifice the real measure of love?
Genuine love in married life comes only
to two people who are mutually
and supremely unselfish.

Father Flanagan

The trick about love is that we get to see
the best part of other people with the best part
of ourselves.

Merritt Malloy

In happiness brought to others,
our own happiness is reflected.

Father Flanagan

Love is blind to blemishes and faults.

Irish Proverb

Love will creep where it cannot go.

Irish Proverb

Love to live...and live to love.

Irish Proverb

True love does not have a happy ending; true love doesn't have an ending.

E.C. McKenzie

10

Community

The Irish bond is strong throughout the world. Among Irish, there exists a sense of belonging to the motherland and to one another. This sense of community is one of Ireland's greatest gifts to the world.

If you are Irish, it may be time to claim your heritage and join the community. If you aren't Irish, you might want to apply for adoption. If so, be sure to apply on St. Patrick's Day. On St. Patrick's day, everyone is lucky enough to be Irish.

There is perpetual kindness
in the Irish cabin.

Sir Walter Scott

Love is never defeated,
and I could add,
the history of Ireland
proves that.

Pope John Paul II

You can stroke people with words.

F. Scott Fitzgerald

There was never a scabby sheep in a flock
that didn't like to have a comrade.

Irish Proverb

Once you have lived with another,
it is great torture to have to live alone.

Carson McCullers

There is no greater need than
the need for a friend.

Irish Proverb

The first rule of orphanages
and Irish families is there's
always room for one more.

Father Francis Mulcahy (M*A*S*H*)

In the new year,
may your right hand
always be stretched out
in friendship and
never in want.

Irish Toast

Observations on Roads, Politics, Fiddles and Other Irish Facts of Life

The following wee bits o' wisdom come to us courtesy of the Emerald Isle. Enjoy!

Nothing is politically right
        that is morally wrong.

Daniel O'Connell

All politics are local.

Tip O'Neill

God does not like a lying tongue.

Irish Proverb

When mistrust comes
in,
Love goes out.

Irish Proverb

Who keeps his tongue
keeps his friend.

Irish Proverb

If you keep your mouth
shut, you will never
put your foot in it.

Austin O'Malley

However long the road,
there comes a turning.

Irish Proverb

The older the fiddle,
the sweeter the tune.

Irish Proverb

May the road rise to
  meet you,
May the wind blow at your
  back,
May the sun shine warm
  upon your face.
May the rains fall soft
  upon your fields,
And until we
  meet again,
May God hold you softly
  in the palm of His hand.

Irish Blessing

Sources

About the Author

Jim Gallery lives and writes in Middle Tennessee. He serves as senior editor for both Brighton Books and Walnut Grove Press. In addition, Jim is a sought-after speaker and lecturer.

Jim is a graduate of the University of South Florida and the New Orleans Baptist Theological Seminary. He is the father of two children. He is also the author of *God Can Handle It*, and *God Can Handle It ...for Teenagers*.

About Wisdom Books

Wisdom Books chronicle memorable quotations in an easy-to-read style. This series provides inspiring, thoughtful and humorous messages from entertainers, athletes, scientists, politicians, clerics, writers and renegades. Each title focuses on a particular region or area of special interest. For more information about these or other books by Walnut Grove Press, please call:

1-(800)-256-8584